MW00570547

51 Ways to Save Your Job

Your 30-Minute Guide to Job Security

By
Paul Timm

CAREER PRESS
180 Fifth Avenue
P.O. Box 34
Hawthorne, NJ 07507
1-800-CAREER-1
201-427-0229 (outside U.S.)
FAX: 201-427-2037

Copyright © 1992 by Paul Timm

51 WAYS TO SAVE YOUR JOB
YOUR 30-MINUTE GUIDE TO JOB SECURITY
ISBN 1-56414-032-6, $6.95

Cover design by Harvey Kraft
Printing by Bookmart Press

To order this title by mail, please include price as noted above, $2.50 handling per order, and $1.00 for each book ordered. Send to: Career Press, Inc., 180 Fifth Ave., P.O. Box 34, Hawthorne, NJ 07507

Or call Toll-free 1-800-CAREER-1 (Canada: 201-427-0229) to order using VISA or MasterCard, or for further information on books from Career Press.

Library of Congress Cataloging-in-Publication Data
Timm, Paul R.
     51 ways to save your job : your 30-minute guide to job security / by Paul Timm.
         p.   cm.
     Includes index.
     ISBN 1-56414-032-6 : $6.95
     1. Vocational guidance. 2. Self-presentation. 3. Job security. I. Title. II. Title : Fifty-one ways to save your job.
HF5381.T5665   1992
650.14--dc20   92-14519
                                          CIP

Contents

Part 2: Focus On Your Attitude

Part 3: Sharpen Your Vision

Part 4: Increase Your Effectiveness

Introduction

You Don't Have To Beat The Bear

Two hikers stumbled upon a huge Grizzly bear. The animal caught their scent and the chase began. After running just a few yards, one hiker suddenly dropped his pack and pulled out a pair of track shoes. His buddy yelled, "Are you crazy? You can't outrun a grizzly." The other hiker just smiled and yelled back, "I don't have to. I just have to outrun you!

Downsizing.
Streamlining.
Trimming the fat.
Automating.
Getting lean and mean.

Every company talks about producing *more* goods at *lower* cost and with *fewer* people. The trends of the 1990s point toward even more emphasis on efficiency. And efficiency usually means cutting the most expensive costs—people costs.

Outplacement.
Force reductions.
De-hiring.
Career readjustment.
Furloughing.

These are all terms that try to soften the bare fact that people are being canned. Fired. Let go. Kicked out.

Trimming the labor force involves choices. Although companies often say they turn to layoffs as a last resort, the facts show otherwise. A survey by Right Associates of 1,240 companies that had reduced staff (reported in the April 14, 1992, *Wall Street Journal*) showed that only 6 percent of these companies tried cutting pay, 9 percent shortened workweeks, and 14 percent developed job sharing plans to save money. The rest—nearly *three quarters* of the companies—went directly to layoffs.

The 1990s is fast becoming the Worry Decade. According to Mark Clements ("What Worries Voters Most," *Parade* Magazine, May 2, 1992), in the past year one person in 10 has been laid off, one person in five has had a family member laid off, and among those who are still employed, more than two out of five work in a company that has laid someone off in the past year.

Most pundits agree that this situation will not change in the foreseeable future. Given this glowing future, the question will not be, "Will your company have layoffs?" It will really boil down to a far more personal question: "When layoffs happen, who will stay and who will go?"

The purpose of this book is to make sure *you* are one of the chosen who stays—if you want to. Using the tactics in this book will give you the choice...and the control over your career in a most uncontrollable time.

Let me make one point clear, up front: I am not talking about groveling to keep your job. I haven't included a section covering basic begging techniques.

What this book *does* do is show you how to boost your *value* to the organization, *any* organization. It teaches a strategy for bullet-proofing your position, for building your value to the organization so that, if downsizing does occur, you'll remain.

In fact, you may even be given greater power as a survivor. You'll be anointed as one of the indispensables.

In short, *you'll save your job.*

"Friendly firings" don't exist. Managers don't enjoy terminating people. It's a gut-wrenching experience for

9

everyone involved. But managers are obligated to make rational choices. Sometimes the difference between who stays and who goes is a very fine line. Like the racer's edge, the difference between winning and losing can often be inches or seconds. You don't have to outrun everybody. But you do need to be better than the people you'll be measured against.

How Vulnerable Are You Now?

How secure is your job? The questionnaire below may give you an idea. (Some of the items in this questionnaire are adapted from a similar survey published in "How to Get Job Security," by Lani Luciano, *Money* magazine, February, 1992. Items have been reworded.)

Choose the one answer to each question that best describes you or your current work situation:

1. The specific work I do is:
     A. Crucial to the organization's success
     B. Of somewhat lower priority
     C. Constantly changing or unpredictable
2. In my last performance appraisal, my work effort and results were rated as:
     A. Good
     B. Unchanged or satisfactory
     C. Needing improvement
     D. Needing *lots* of improvement
3. I know there are:
     A. People above me in the organization who do not like me
     B. People below me in the organization who do not like me
     C. No people at work who dislike me

4. My mentor (that is, the person who supports my career efforts and helps me achieve them):
    A. Is riding high in the company
    B. Has fallen from favor
    C. Doesn't exist; I don't have one

5. My boss:
    A. Likes me
    B. Doesn't like me
    C. Doesn't know who I am

6. My reputation extends:
    A. Beyond my company to other companies
    B. Beyond my department to other parts of my organization
    C. To the water cooler

7. The last time I learned a new skill was:
    A. During the past year
    B. When I started my job
    C. In school

8. The way I feel about my job is best described as:
    A. Enthusiastic
    B. Indifferent
    C. Worried

9. Within the past 18 months, my company:
    A. Bought another company
    B. Was bought by another company
    C. Stayed the same

10. The people who started with the company at the same time I did have since:
    A. Advanced or moved up a level
    B. Lost responsibilities or left the company
    C. Stayed at the same level as when they started.

Add or subtract points for your answers using the table on p. 13. Then total your score for all questions.

If you scored 15 or more points, your job is probably solid. You can use the ideas in this book to strengthen your hold and advance your career.

If you scored between 10 and 14 points, you could be in good shape, but may want to polish up your weak spots.

A score between 5 and 9 points should serve as an early warning signal—it's time for a self-examination.

If you scored between 1 and 4 points, you are probably on shaky ground.

Zero points or less? Type up your resume...tonight.

Using the Power of E-Plus

This book is based on what I call an "E-Plus Strategy." The letter E stands for **Expectations**—what your employer or manager expects from you. You create a *"Plus"* when you exceed these expectations in some way. You don't have to exceed them by a mile—often just a few inches will do. In fact, it's often the little things that make all the difference when a tough choice must be made to reduce staff.

So let's start with this premise: **It's The Little Things That Make The Difference.**

The little things add up. A single wire may snap under a relatively light load, but a cable made of many strands of the same wire can hold up tons. Like adding strand upon strand of wire, your actions over time make your cable immeasurably stronger.

What *kinds* of little things? That's what the rest of this book is about. These little things fall into four categories that, coincidentally, spell out the word SAVE:

Skills

Attitudes

Values

Effectiveness

This book is your workbook for success. It is based on a sound philosophy and psychologically proven principles. You will learn how to create a strategy for *career* fulfillment as well as *job* security.

So let's get on with those *51 Ways To Save Your Job.*

How to Score Your Test

Add or subtract the following points for each answer:

1A:	+3	4A:	+3	7B:	+1
1B:	+1	4B:	-1	7C:	-2
1C	-1	4C:	0	8A:	+3
2A:	+1	5A:	+3	8B:	-1
2B:	0	5B:	-1	8C:	-3
2C:	-1	5C:	0	9A:	-1
2D:	-3	6A:	+3	9B:	-3
3A:	-3	6B:	+2	9C:	0
3B:	-1	6C:	-1	10A:	-3
3C:	0	7A:	+3	10B:	0
				10C:	+3

Part 1

Develop Your Skills

1

Find Your
Leverage Points

In the old days, men working in the railroad yards moved large rail cars by hand. Well, not exactly by *hand*— pushing a car was beyond even the toughest man. What one man could do, however, was use a large stick as a lever under the wheels of the car. With no more than leverage power, one man *could* move a railroad car!

Some things you do at work produce results far beyond what you may realize. These tasks add value to the company at a reasonable cost.

A self-inventory can identify your leverage points—the points where you make the most impact. Here is a quick way to find leverage points. Answer these questions:

1. What do I do better than most others?
2. What can I do more quickly or efficiently than others?
3. What tasks do I enjoy most at work?
4. When do I contribute most heavily to my organization's goals?

These are your leverage-point tasks. Now look for opportunities to use your best skills. Offer to do these tasks. Get that leverage working for you.

Speaking before groups was one task I was pretty good at. I enjoyed it. I was a bit of a ham, and my audiences seemed to like me. So early in my career as a manager trainee with a telephone company I offered to handle the requests that came in periodically for a guest speaker. I ended up speaking to many civic groups and organizations. My boss and the other managers were delighted—they, like many people, *hated* public speaking. And they were impressed by my initiative, abilities (outside my "at work" duties) and readiness to help out.

Another example: While a college student, I spent summers as a "kitchen boy" at a local camp. The other fellows hated the job of washing the pots and pans. Normally the crew rotated jobs, but I volunteered to be the "professional" pots and pans guy.

The others probably thought I was a little nuts. I looked at it as taking on a "lemon" of a job and learning how to make lemonade. I searched for the positive aspects of the job, and found them surprisingly plentiful: I could work at my own pace, listen to the radio as I worked, and flirt with the waitresses on a steady basis. I quickly became a specialist!

Take a job inventory to identify *your* leverage points. Then offer to maximize your value to the company by using your best skills.

2
Get *Really* Good
At What You Do

When I was a kid thinking about what I wanted to do when I grew up, my dad would always say, "Son, no

matter what you decide to be, be the best one there is."
You've probably heard such advice. Dad (and many dads
like him) had learned something important: There is
great satisfaction in being *really* good at what you do.

The bottom line of job security lies in having the skills
companies or people will pay you for. People get paid for
doing things that need to be done, and doing them *well*.

Some job skills are always in demand. Good salespeo-
ple and computer wizards, for example, will always be
able to sift through a pile of job offers. Why? Because a lot
of people just aren't cut out for sales or prefer to avoid it.
And, for many of us, our eyes glaze over when we even
have to talk about computers. Other jobs go unfilled
because they require special talents or levels of education
that most of us don't have.

Ask yourself this question regularly: "Why would
anyone *pay* me for doing what I do?" Your answer will
help you identify what your value really is.

People pay others to do things they cannot or choose not
to do themselves. They are willing to give you good money
for doing things they are too busy doing other tasks to do;
they don't know how to do; or you can do more efficiently
than they can.

You increase your job security by continually learning
ways to do such tasks quicker and better. Look for good
shortcuts. Look for ways to continually improve quality. If
you make small, incremental improvements every day, no
one will be able to catch you. You'll be more valuable to the
company today than yesterday, even more tomorrow.

Look for your niche—the area where you can make the
greatest contribution. Then commit to becoming the best.
Regular practice or daily study of your chosen niche can
quickly make you the expert. Spend 20 minutes a day—

every day—reading and building skills in your niche and within six months you'll have the equivalent of a college degree in that specialty. Spend a year focused on it and you'll be a national expert.

3
Invest In *Yourself*

Companies increase their stock's value when they invest in equipment and employees. You can increase *your* value by investing in *yourself.* The employee who works to constantly improve his or her knowledge and skills grows in value to the company.

Two kinds of personal investment make sense: in **self-maintenance** and **skill development.**

Self-maintenance can be physical fitness (regular involvement in athletics or other physical exercise) and mental/emotional fitness (like classes in self-management, stress reduction, and the like).

Your investment can take many forms. While some money may be involved, it is far more important to invest some *time.* Here are a few ideas for investing in your skills:

- **Join a health club** or participate in regular athletic activity.
- **Attend seminars or lectures** on topics of interest to you. Often such programs are

19

offered at little or no cost through colleges, community associations, hospital-patient education programs, and others.

- *Set a goal to read a certain number of books.* Discuss what you've read with others.
- *Attend a concert, opera, play, tractor pull, rodeo.* Try something new!

Why bother? Having a broad range of activities helps you on the job in two ways. First, all knowledge can be potentially useful and should be valued for itself. You can come up with the darnedest ideas for on-the-job improvement from the most unlikely sources.

Second, a wide range of activities gives you breadth. Breadth gives you things to talk to people about. The good conversationalist ultimately has the advantage over the tongue-tied person who can talk only about sports or the kids.

4

Develop Excellent Customer Skills

Everybody has customers—they are either the end users of your products or services or other people in the organization who depend upon you. Great customer service is the master key to career success.

In my previous book, *50 Simple Things You Can Do To Save Your Customers* (Career Press, 1992, $6.95), I stressed that E-Plus is especially applicable to customer service. In fact, the key to keeping your customers and building a successful business is *to understand customer expectations and then exceed them.*

Sharpen your customer skills by constantly putting yourself in the shoes of your customers and seeking to understand what they expect from you. Then, exceed those expectations in some ways.

The ways to exceed can be remembered by the acronym VIS-PAC—your goal is to make a **VIS**ible **PAC**kage of benefits to your customer:

Value Exceed expectations by giving *more value* than your customer expects to get from your product or service. (Examples: Make it last longer and be more reliable, easier to use, etc.)

Information Give *more information* than expected or provide useful information in a format that is easier to use. (Examples: Include an instruction sheet, videotape instructions, color code parts.)

Speed Provide your services *faster* than expected. (Example: Federal Express promises to deliver by 10 a.m. but often shows up at 9:30 or even earlier. Under-promise; over-deliver.)

Price Estimate prices and then come in a bit *cheaper*. The "$200 brake job on your car" that actually costs you $191.75 is a pleasant surprise that builds customer loyalty. The $220 bill does not create an E-Plus.

Add-on   *Give away* something to your cus-
                    tomers. A candy jar on your desk,
                    free popcorn with a video rental, free
                    car wash with a fill-up are examples.

Convenience   Offer to *deliver or pick up* something.
                    Help customers carry things to the
                    car, offer auto services at customer
                    homes, etc. These are examples of E-
                    Plus in convenience.

The point: Be constantly on the lookout for E-Plus opportunities and take advantage of them. You'll keep your customers coming back and build your value to the company.

5

Read Publications About Your Job Or Industry

Keep current with what's happening in your profession and industry. Read the latest information. Then clip or photocopy articles that could be of interest to your boss or work associates and send them along with a note from you.

The result: You are seen as one who is truly interested in the business *and* as a coworker willing to share ideas of value.

The lower your level in the organization, the more impact this can have. As an entry-level worker, for example, few bosses would expect you to do this. That poses a perfect E-Plus opportunity. Take advantage of it.

6
Communicate Gratitude
In Writing

When I was a manager trainee in my early 20s, I sent a letter to the college recruiter who had hired me. The letter was brief—it simply said how much I enjoyed working for the company and how he had helped me. I received a call from him a few days later. He thanked me for the letter and commented that of all the trainees he had worked with, I was the only one who had written to him in this way.

Interestingly, a short while later he was instrumental in my getting promoted to a better position.

Harvey Mackay talks about "short notes [that] yield long results" in his book, ***Swim With the Sharks Without Being Eaten***. He comments on how few people send follow-up notes to customers, even those who have made a major purchase, like a car. Have you received a thank-you note from a business lately?

I remember getting a handwritten note of thanks from the owner of a sports shoe store a few years ago. His message simply said thanks for shopping with us and we appreciate your business. Why would I remember such a note? Because it was the only one I ever received from *any* business. That manager used E-Plus. He exceeded my expectations and won a loyal customer.

Mackay cites many successful people who constantly send out short but effective notes with messages like "I want you to know how much I enjoyed our meeting/your gift/your hospitality" or "Congratulations on your new house/car/tennis trophy."

The moral of the story: Don't hesitate to let people know that you appreciate them, and do it *in writing*. Don't worry too much about grammar or business letter format. Often a handwritten note works fine. Just do it.

7

Become
Multi-Competent

There is always a place in the company for the person who says "I'll take care of it"...and *does*.

The more different tasks you can "take care of," the more valuable you become. This may seem to conflict with the earlier recommendation that you find a niche and become a specialist, but it doesn't need to. Become an expert at what you do *now* while also looking for opportunities to develop related skills that can be used in other situations.

"If you ride the same winning horse for too long, people will start to wonder about the rest of your stable," says

Mark McCormack, author of **What They Don't Teach You at the Harvard Business School.**

For example, if your current job is to prepare bills, see what you can also learn about collection techniques. If you handle customer complaints, expand your skills to include sales, too. If you drive a delivery truck, learn how the warehouse is organized and how inventory controls work. Develop a natural curiosity—ask people how things work.

Company management training programs will rotate trainees through experiences in virtually all departments in the organization. This makes trainees more versatile and also allows them to discover their best talents. If you are not in such a training program, just create your own —through curiosity, questions and reading.

The utility player—one capable of playing any number of different positions on a baseball team—can be a company's most valuable player.

One further benefit: If it does become necessary to change jobs, your wide range of experiences will qualify you for a wider range of positions.

8
Build Your
Listening Skills

A friend of mine is hard of hearing. At lunch one day he told me about this marvelous new hearing aid he had.

"It hides completely in the ear. I can hear a pin drop from across the room," he enthused.

"Really?" I asked. "What kind is it?"

"2:45," he answered, looking at his watch.

My friend is no worse off than people who can hear fine but just don't *listen*. Of all the communication skills, listening is the most important. Few people do it well. With a little effort and some practice, you can become an exceptional listener. Here are some tips:

First, decide which type of listening is called for: **support listening** or **retention listening.**

Use *support listening* when people need you for encouragement, understanding or sympathy. They may not even want any solutions from you, just a sounding board to express themselves. In these cases, focus on listening to learn what that person thinks and feels.

To do this better, use three responses:

> ***Open-ended questions:*** Use questions that cannot be answered with a simple yes, no or one-word answer. Phrase questions so that the respondent must elaborate: "What has you so upset?" rather than, "Are you upset?"

> ***"Uh-huh" response:*** Use noncommittal phrases such as "uh-huh," "hmmm," or "I can see what you mean" to get people to continue explaining their views. Accompany these comments with a nod or other nonverbal expression of agreement.

> ***Content reflection:*** Repeat back what you heard to get confirmation and elaboration on a point. Repeat what was said in a tone of voice that does not imply disagreement.

The dialogue below shows the use of the three support listening techniques.

Rene: Danny, how do you feel about the department? *(Open-ended question)*

Danny: Working in this department is extremely difficult.

Rene: Uh-huh. *(Uh-huh response)*

Danny: What I mean is that I have trouble getting along with Doris.

Rene: Hmmm. *(Uh-huh response)*

Danny: She just can't accept the fact that I'm her supervisor.

Rene: Doris can't accept you as her boss? *(Content reflection)*

Danny: That's right! She makes snide remarks about working for a "kid."

Rene: What kinds of things does she say? *(Open-ended question)*

I think you can see how Rene will quickly and easily identify the exact problem she needs to solve.

Retention listening uses different techniques. Here the goal is to remember the information presented for possible later use. To do so, you must pay close attention and organize the ideas mentally for future reference.

But don't feel you have to rely just on your memory—even better than a good memory is a pencil and paper. Make notes of what is said. Practice good note-taking techniques and use them. People will be flattered and reassured when they see you taking notes about what they are saying.

And your notes won't forget!

9

Treat *All* People Well

During my friend Alan's first year of business, he faced a budget problem that forced him to eliminate a job. Clara had been hired to drive a truck and deliver parts. Her position paid minimum wage, but she enjoyed it.

When Alan realized he couldn't afford even minimum wage, he spent hours calling other business people to help Clara find a new job. She went to work elsewhere and was happy. And she appreciated Alan's efforts on her behalf.

Six months later, Clara's grandmother died and left her $8 million. Because of Alan's earlier helpfulness, she went back to him to ask if she could invest in his business. What goes around comes around!

10

Know How & When To Run A Meeting

For better or for worse, most companies are run by meetings. Properly organized, planned and executed, meetings are advantageous to both the organization and the people who participate. Run poorly, and meetings become a huge waste of time.

If you are called on to lead a meeting, remember these helpful tips:

1. Be sure the meeting is really needed. There are only two reasons to have a meeting, *any* meeting: To develop new ideas that people wouldn't come up with working alone, and to gain acceptance of the decision once made (people involved in making a decision seldom fight its implementation). The drawbacks to using meetings are their high cost (especially in "people time") and the poor-quality decisions that can result if the group doesn't work freely or efficiently.

2. Invite only participants who have an interest in the topic.

3. Prepare an agenda and stick to it.

4. Allow give-and-take but not domination of the group. If one person or faction is railroading the group, step in and draw out the rest of the participants.

5. Avoid scheduling meetings as a substitute for action. "Meeting" a problem to death does not solve it.

6. Avoid the meetings-as-a-social-experience or holding a 10:00 a.m. meeting every Tuesday because "we *always* have a 10:00 a.m. meeting on Tuesdays."

7. Always ask if this meeting is worth its cost. A dozen people meeting for a few hours can quickly add up to a lot of money!

11

Know How To Participate In A Meeting

When invited to a meeting or discussion, come prepared. Ask for an agenda in advance (or at least clarification of what will be covered). Find out why you are invited—what your role is. Then do your homework.

Here are some other tips for better meeting participation:

- Get there a few minutes *early,* refreshed and ready to work.

- *Sit* opposite the leader. You'll get more involved and be noticed.

- Stay *focused* on the topic. Write it in bold letters on your note paper. Help the leader keep on track.

- *Avoid* getting into side conversations, dominating the discussion, interrupting the meeting, or getting overly emotional.

- Be *open and supportive* of the ideas of others. *Listen* actively. Ask clarifying questions. Express approval when appropriate.

- Try to *help the leader control* the meeting. If arguments break out, try to clarify both points of view objectively. If the group wanders off the topic, suggest that it refocus on the key question.

- *Pay attention.* Take notes. Be an *active* participant. Try to make the process as effective as possible (even if you would prefer not to be in the meeting at all!)

12
Know When & How To "Loosen Up"

When you work, work hard. When you play or goof off, do that with enthusiasm, too. The harder you work, the more you need to "recharge"—your work will be better if you can get the breaks you need on a consistent basis

In Las Vegas casinos, dealers take a break every 20 minutes—managers recognize the pressure these people are under. Even "people who need people" sometimes need a break from people.

13
Be Aware Of Your Nonverbal Messages

The vast majority of what we communicate to people has nothing to do with the words spouting out of our mouths. We communicate with body position, tone of voice, posture, dress, timing and countless other subtle cues. How important are these nonverbal communications? When your actions contradict your words, people will always believe the nonverbal message.

If you stand too close, you'll be considered pushy; too far away and you'll seem aloof. If you sit behind a huge desk while visitors sit across from you on chairs two feet lower than yours, you'll convey dominance. If you dress sloppily, you'll be perceived as being unaware of quality.

Nonverbal communication doesn't always convey an accurate message. I know sloppy dressers whose work is always accurate and meticulous, outwardly stuffy fellows who are really sensitive and caring, and super-friendly gladhanders who would steal your child's favorite toy without a thought. You can't always trust the nonverbals, but people will...until proven wrong.

Study "body language" and nonverbal meanings and anticipate how you may be coming across to others. Think about the image you project.

Jeffery Davidson, in his book *Blow Your Own Horn*, suggests checking your image this way: Make three blank copies of the following list. On one copy, describe yourself in each category. Under "shoes," for example, you might describe your typical shoes as "black, slightly worn heels with scuff marks on top." Or under the category "posture, bearing," you might describe your normal posture as "erect but not rigid." Then list what you think each self-description conveys to other people. Using the shoe example, you may write that your typical shoes convey a careless attitude.

After filling out the form, Davidson suggests that you give one copy to a coworker you trust and one copy to your spouse or a close friend. Ask them to write the same information about you, a description and what this conveys. Use the three perceptions to analyze your image.

Personal Appearance

Wardrobe   _____

Suit   _____

Shirt/blouse   _____

Ties/scarves   _____

Belt   _____

Shoes   _____

Glasses   _____

Jewelry/watch   _____

Briefcase   _____

Personal

Hairstyle   _____

Fingernails   _____

Beard/moustache   _____

Makeup   _____

Body Language   _____

Accessories

Type of pen   _____

Purse/wallet   _____

Business cards   _____

Cigarettes/cigars/
chewing gum   _____

Physical characteristics

Posture/bearing _____

Facial expression _____

Nervous habits _____

Hand gestures _____

Eye contact _____

Personal space _____

Touch _____

Voice characteristics

Rate of speech _____

Loudness _____

Pitch _____

Nasality _____

Resonance _____

Automobile

Year, make _____

Exterior condition _____

Interior condition _____

Office/work area

Decor/pictures _____

Overall cleanliness _____

Overall orderliness _____

Furniture positioning _____

14

Learn How To Manage Your Boss

Bosses give orders, and subordinates carry them out, right? Well, not always. We expect the manager to describe the project that needs to be done, make assignments, then check the completed work. When bosses don't behave this way—and often they don't—workers get confused. Tension, conflicts, missed deadlines, and employee turnover can result.

Remember: Bosses are not mind readers. And more often than not, they *are* human! They make mistakes. The more you protect his or her job by doing what needs to be done—whether or not your boss can figure it out—the more valuable you are to that boss and to the organization.

Sit down with your boss and ask what he or she expects from you. Listen carefully and take notes. List not only job activities but also job *purposes*. A good way to do this is to write the job activity and then continue each statement with "in order to..." and try to complete the sentence. This will give you a clearer picture of what should be accomplished and *why*.

If your boss has some trouble being explicit about these job assignments, write out your own draft and ask if he or she agrees.

Once job content is clarified, two other key issues should be discussed in a similar manner: ***How much initiative does your boss want you to take?*** When can you go ahead and make decisions and when should you check in advance? *How much does your boss want to be kept informed?* Should you carry assignments through to completion or check in periodically to report progress?

15

Use Cost-Benefit Reasoning

Someone defined insanity as "finding something that doesn't work...and doing more of it!"

Cost-benefit reasoning simply means clarifying what the results we are achieving are actually costing us in time, effort, money, etc. If the benefits don't outweigh the costs (or at least have the *potential* to exceed the costs in the future), it is probably irrational to continue to produce those results.

Recent research at the University of Michigan has shown that people who use cost-benefit analysis in their everyday lives are more successful. Economists have long preached the importance of such analysis in predicting consumer behavior and the like. But it has wider application.

The Michigan study quizzed faculty members and university seniors on such questions as how often they walked out of a bad movie, refused to finish a bad meal, scrapped a weak term paper or abandoned a research project that was going nowhere. The researchers believed that people who cut their losses this way were following sound economic rules by calculating net benefits of alternative courses of action, writing off past costs that couldn't be recovered, and weighing the opportunity to use future time and effort more profitably elsewhere.

The findings: Faculty members who used such cost-benefit reasoning earned higher salaries than those who didn't. Students who used cost-benefit analysis earned higher grades that their Scholastic Aptitude Test scores would have predicted.

The skill of cost-benefit reasoning can help determine where to put forth effort for maximum effect. The result: increased productivity.

16

Avoid Perfection Paralysis

My friend Sid was working as a salesman to earn some money to finish his Ph.D. His postgraduate course-work was completed, and he had passed his comprehensive exams. All that remained was to write his dissertation.

The topic was approved, and Sid was ready to go. But he never went. He just couldn't write.

As he discussed his problem with me, I couldn't help but remember the line by famed sportswriter Red Smith: "Writing is easy: All you have to do is sit at your typewriter until little drops of blood appear on your forehead."

Well, that's where Sid sat. But nothing happened.

His problem was a fairly common one—his expectations were out of whack. He harbored the misconception that when writing appears on paper it should be perfect. He couldn't seem to get the concept of the *rough* draft through his otherwise intelligent brain. He demanded a perfection from himself that was simply impossible.

I finally convinced him to scribble down some rough draft ideas, even if they weren't complete thoughts. Write *something*. Then fix it later. That's the way people write. Nobody gets it perfect the first (or even the second, or third or fourth) time around.

People who relentlessly chase perfection are chasing a wily coyote. Perfection is an illusion, perhaps humankind's ultimate illusion. The harder we try for it, the more disappointed we will eventually be.

The compulsive perfection-seeker not only suffers paralysis like Sid, but can also face stress-related health problems, troubled relationships (who wants to be around such a person?) and low self-esteem.

17
Avoid Reverse Delegation & Creative Incompetence

Sometimes we should accept delegation—when it's part of our job or it'll help the project move along—other times we should not. One common ploy used by people who don't want to do what they should is the plea of *creative incompetence.*

My wife has a clever way of getting me to do things around the house. She begins the project and then feigns incompetence. We needed to install some new curtain rods a few months ago. After climbing up the ladder and drilling some holes—she was doing a great job—the phone rang and she suddenly realized that she didn't have the ability to do this job after all. "You'll finish this up for my, won't you dear?" she called as she headed out the door.

I used the time manager's magic word—"No." Unfortunately, she didn't hear me. After I finished hanging the curtain rods, I promised myself I wouldn't be tricked into doing someone else's work again. Needless to say, it's a hard promise to keep.

There's an old saying that goes, "If you do a job twice, it's yours." The assistant who offers to go for coffee quickly becomes the coffee go-fer. The fellow who stops by the print shop on his way to the office will become the print shop go-fer. Job descriptions get rewritten and expanded by such volunteerism.

Be wary of doing other people's work for them. Your work will suffer. Worse, it may expand into areas you don't want it to.

Part 2

Focus On
Your Attitudes

18

Focus On The Here & Now

The past is totally uncontrollable. The future may be influenced by what we do now, but we can't control it either. So that leaves the "now"—the only unit of time we can work with. Don't look back. We've all made mistakes, we've all done stupid things, we've all stumbled at one time or another. But what's done is done—agonizing over the past won't do any good.

The great challenge is to stay in the now. Focus your time and energies on what you can do *now*. And *enjoy* it now. It's fine to set a goal to move up in your company, but the best way to reach that goal some tomorrow is to do a great job *today*.

19

Understand Your Core Values

Our values are the things we've decided are most worth giving ourselves to. They define what we see as worthwhile. They describe what we should be giving our time, energy and efforts to. Personal values need no outside validation to justify their desirability. They are strictly individual, although we must be wary of values that are anti-social or destructive to others. The person who gets a warm feeling about the value of armed robbery will meet stiff resistance and may spend a life of getting frustrated (or rotting in jail).

How do you know what your values are?

Imagine that someone placed a 10-foot long plank on the floor and asked you to walk across it. If you did, he'd give you $10. Would you do it? You probably would.

What if that same plank were placed between the tops of two skyscrapers. Would you still walk across it for $10? For $100? $10,000? Most people probably wouldn't try even if the sum were $1 million.

But what if the plank were between the skyscrapers and your *child* was standing on the other end. Now the man said, "Either you cross to your child...or your child has to walk to you."

What do you think the typical response would be now? Not surprisingly, most folks would say they would readily risk their lives to save their child. That reaction is the beginning of a definition of a **core value.** Many of us would readily risk our lives for—or give our lives to—our children. They are worth any sacrifice we can make for their well-being. Even walking the plank!

Value-directed people talk about values, often citing stories of how they (or others) acted in ways congruent with those bone-deep beliefs. The British Olympic runner in the movie *Chariots of Fire,* who refused to compete on the Sabbath—even when asked to by royalty—made a powerful statement about his religious values. He drew the line; his personal ethic was clear.

It is the value-based activities that are worth sticking with and putting your whole self into. You'll do so cheerfully because of their importance to you. By applying your precious and limited time and effort to those things that make a difference, you'll learn to work smarter, not just harder. Given a realistic perception of control, a clear set of values, and persistent effort to become one with those values, you cannot fail.

As motivational speaker Denis Waitley puts it in his book *The Double Win:* "The vast majority live by default, not knowing where they want to go, having no need to figure out how to get there. Not specifying their goals, they have no plans to follow, no new habits to develop, no behaviors to rehearse, and no strate-gies to revise and update..."

20
Maintain Positive Self-Esteem

Building your self-esteem is a do-it-to-yourself project.

Step 1: Talk To Yourself

Give yourself a pat on the back for a job well done. Compliment yourself; applaud your achievements. Say it out loud.

We all talk to ourselves constantly. Unfortunately, most of what we say is negative and works against us.

With a little discipline, we can turn the tables on the negative and use positive self-talk to our advantage. Just listen to what you are saying to yourself. Then change it to be positive, upbeat and optimistic.

When you do succeed at something—*any*thing—give yourself a verbal pat on the back for a job well done.

In addition to complimenting yourself on specific things, make it a point to simply say, "I like myself" at least 25 times a day. It sounds a little weird, but trust me—it's OK. In fact, it's very healthy.

Step 2: Demand Respect

Those around you will treat you with as much respect as you demand. We attract to ourselves the kinds of people and circumstances that *we feel we deserve*. We each deserve respect, so don't allow yourself to be treated with anything less.

Develop some assertiveness skills. Speak up when you have an opinion. Diplomatically but firmly make yourself heard. Understand, however, that assertiveness is not aggressiveness. My favorite definition of assertiveness is "being pleasantly direct." Express feelings honestly.

Name-calling isn't assertiveness. In fact, it produces more heat than light. For example, if someone offends you, don't say, "Pete, you're a jerk" (even though that may be true). Instead say, "Pete, what you are saying makes me angry." That's assertiveness.

Step 3: Teach Others To Treat You Well

Let people know that you want them to tell you when they notice things about you that they *like* as well as when they notice things that irritate or concern them.

45

A sample discussion with your boss, for example, might sound like this: "Boss, I realize that it's part of your job to correct me when I'm doing something wrong, but could I ask a small favor? Would you also let me know when I'm on the *right* track? That would help me do a better job and make me feel good, too.

Few people could refuse such a reasonable request.

Step 4: Tell Others What You Like About Them

Check to see if you are much quicker to offer "constructive criticism" than a compliment. If so, try forcing the reverse. Walk up to someone you've known for a long time and offer a nice compliment. Make it sincere and specific. Then walk away. They may be confused at first, but they'll like it, and you'll feel good, too.

Make it a daily goal to compliment someone. You'll make another person's day and create a winning cycle that will surely come back to you.

When you begin to comment on the positive traits and actions of others, you'll boost their self-esteem. The better they feel about themselves, the more likely they will also feed *your* self-confidence.

Step 5: Remind Yourself That You Really Are Good At Some Things

Accept yourself unconditionally as a being of great worth. Validate your self-worth through your accomplishments, too. It make sense to "positivize" your image of yourself by discovering your strengths and talents. Remember, nobody is good at *every*thing, but everybody is good at *some*thing.

Take a personal inventory of your current and potential skills and talents. Spend some uninterrupted time listing all the things you are good at or could *become* good at. Force yourself to make the list as long as possible. Fill up several sheets—a whole tablet of paper if possible—with your talents and potentials. Doing this can help identify the most fruitful areas for further building of your self-confidence.

Next, identify three to five things from your list that you really want to be good at. Be sure these are things you'd be willing to devote time and effort to. Learn to focus your time on your talent areas, on the activities that give you the most satisfaction. As you get better at these activities, you'll give yourself the best self-confidence builders and attract the admiration of others. People like to be around winners.

The more time you can spend using your talents, the faster you will experience positive strides in your confidence growth. The payoff will be virtually immediate. Nothing develops self-esteem as quickly as developing talents and skills.

Step 6: Overcome The Fear Of Failure

The root cause of fear is uncertainty and anticipation of some dreaded outcome. Lee Iacocca talks about his father who used to ask, "Lido, what were you really worried about a month ago? Six months ago? A year ago?" When Lee couldn't even remember, the old man had made his point.

The things we worry about most often don't happen at all. All that good worrying goes to waste. Cross the problem bridges when you come to them. Don't worry in advance or agonize over the past. Live in the here and *now*.

Try this: Jot down two or three things you were really worried about a year ago, six months ago, five years ago. What happened? If you are having a hard time recalling examples, please note that Mr. Iacocca and I are taking a bow.

Step 7: Make Your "Comfort Zone" Bigger

While the fear of failure is a common problem, the fear of *success* hounds many people, too. If your self-concept doesn't allow you to see yourself as a success, and you get there, you'll be outside your psychological "comfort zone." Make your comfort zone bigger.

Most of us have a mental image of how much money we are worth, for example. Some people see themselves as $30,000 a year folks; others as $300,000 a year. Often there is little difference in ability between the two!

One reason people who have made big money *keep* making big money—even if they lost their shirt somewhere along the way—is that they see themselves as being worth the kind of money they made in the past. You can't tell a sales rep who made $150,000 last year that she can't meet or beat that figure this year. She just won't *believe* you.

Even if we haven't made big money in the past, we can program our minds to see ourselves as, for example, a $200,000 a year guy or gal. Use self-talk and visualization to expand your comfort zone and create new possibilities.

Step 8: Reframe Your Thoughts

We really do control the way we look at events. Some people naturally see the bright side of almost everything;

others see the dark side. Reframing is the process of changing a negative perception to a more useful one.

Below is a list of common, everyday situations. How do you see them, positively or negatively?

An active, noisy child

Negative framing: That kid's annoying; maybe he's hyperactive; I wish his parents would do something about him

Positive framing: That's an active, healthy kid. Even though he's a little loud, it's good to see a child having fun.

Being terminated from a job

Negative framing: I'm worried sick. Where will the money come from? I'm too old to start over. This is a disaster

Positive framing: This is a challenge that could work out nicely. I don't have to worry about that long commute any more; I've always wanted to try my hand at ____. This could be a good opportunity to move—maybe now I'll start my own business.

Experiencing a mild heart attack

Negative framing: That scared the hell out of me. I know it's just a matter of time before I'll be struck down again. I hate getting old.

Positive framing: That was a warning. I guess I've been running in the fast lane too long. I'll develop much better health habits now and enjoy a long, full life.

We can't control what *happens* to us but we can *always* control how we react. We choose how we wish to "frame" our experiences.

What Yogi Berra once said about baseball is also true of self-confidence: "95 percent of the game is half mental."

21

Keep A
Positive Outlook

Syndicated columnist Charley Reese writes: "Two days in a row negative people regaled me with their negativism. You know the type. You remark that it's a nice sunny day, and they mention the ozone layer is going. You remark that it's fortunate we're having rain because it's been so dry, and they say it's acid rain. Bite into a good piece of beef, and they will talk about chemical injections and cholesterol and cows blowing methane bubbles into the atmosphere and starving children in the Sudan. Fish, of course, has mercury in it. Vegetables are full of pesticides."

Don't you just love being around people like this? Negativism rests on the unrealistic assumption that a perfect answer or solution exists for any problem. When a less than perfect answer is proposed, negative people reject it.

It's easy to let the world get you down. The real challenge is to remain positive in our negative world. People who learn to do this are far more successful.

Use reframing to shift your view of the world. Look to the bright side, hold out hope, and make the most of the hand you've been dealt.

Motivational speaker Charlie Jones says it best: "The most challenging thing you'll ever face in your life is learning every day to be excited about what you are doing."

22

Foster An Attitude Of Concern For Others

Some people have more natural empathy than others —they really care about all people, even strangers, and become discouraged when others face difficulties. Other people feel that although we've all been dealt a different hand in life's poker game, we need to make the best of it via our own initiative.

Here is a self-test to gauge your natural sense of concern for others. There are no right or wrong answers. Look at each pair of statements below and assign a score that totals 10. If you agree with the A statement much more strongly that the B statement, you may give the A statement a 9 and the B a 1, or the A, 8, and the B, 2.. If you agree with both statements about equally, you would score it 5/5. Remember: Your total score for each pair must equal 10:

1A I am almost always upbeat, in a good mood.   ____
1B My moods vary widely; sometimes I'm grumpy. ____

2A I genuinely enjoy serving other people. ____
2B I'd rather see people help themselves. ____

3A My appearance is important to people I deal with. ____
3B The way I look shouldn't have any effect on other people. ____

4A I smile most of the time. ____
4B I tend to look more serious. ____

5A I love to see people enjoy themselves. ____
5B I don't care much if people I don't know enjoy themselves. ____

6A I try to remember and use people's names. ____
6B Remembering names (especially of people I may never see again) isn't important. ____

7A I take pride in my ability to talk to all kinds of people. ____
7B I talk comfortably with some kinds of people but not others. ____

8A I feel that I represent my company to everyone I deal with. ____
8B It is unfair for people to judge the whole company by what I do. ____

9A I don't mind apologizing on behalf of my company, even when the problem was not my fault. ____
9B It bothers me to have to apologize for something I didn't do. ____

10A I hope that everyone I serve will return to do business with me. ____
10B I don't care if the people I deal with come back or not. ____

Total A scores:_____   Total B scores: _____

The higher your A scores, the higher your concern for others. For customer-contact people, the A scores should be at least *twice* as high as the B scores.

If your sense of concern is lower than you'd like, what can you do? First and most importantly, learn to *empathize*. Put yourself in the shoes of the people you deal with. Remember that they are often on strange turf and may well feel uncertain about how to deal with you.

We all experience these kinds of uncertainty. Remember your first day on a new job? It's uncomfortable for most of us. Likewise, people dealing with you may feel uncomfortable. To boost your value, boost your attitudes of concern. Empathize and act accordingly.

23
Develop Flexibility & Change-Hardiness

In his book, ***Tough-Minded Management*** (AMACOM, 1978), Joe Batten makes a great point about flexibility: "If I place two pieces of material the same size, shape and form on an anvil, and one is made of granite, the other of leather, and then hit each with a hammer, what will happen? The granite will shatter into pieces, precisely *because* it is hard. It is rigid, brittle and weak. The leather is barely dented, precisely because it is *not* hard. It is flexible, malleable, elastic, supple—it is tough."

Flexibility is critical. The world around us is constantly changing, just as we are. After all, you once weighed about eight pounds, and your company was once a start-up operation. "Change-hardiness" is your ability to adapt to new conditions.

Some people spend their time pining for the past. Nostalgia is fine in moments of quiet reflection, but it never helps deal with today. Maybe you recall with fond memories the days when you knew each of your customers, the office reverberated with the clicking of electric typewriters, and the parking was plentiful. Fine. But things have changed, and we need to adapt.

Don't waste emotional energy wishing things were different.

24

Love Your Work

A farmer purchased a prize-winning rooster for $500. His neighbors thought he was crazy. "Five-hundred dollars is a ridiculous price for a rooster," they told him. But soon the farmer saw his investment pay off. Amorously speaking, the rooster started doing what roosters are supposed to do. The farmer noticed that the hens seemed much happier and laid lots of eggs. Within a few weeks, even the turkeys and the ducks were happier and more productive!

One day, while on his way back from town, he was alarmed to see a flock of buzzards circling over something lying in the road. As he came closer, his fears were confirmed. His prize rooster was lying in the road. "Now he's done it," sighed the farmer. "He worked too darned hard."

The farmer rushed up to him and lifted his limp head. The rooster quietly opened one eye, glared at the farmer, and harshly whispered, "What do you think you're doing? You'll scare the buzzards away!"

Love your work. Persistently.

25
Make Your Positive Attitude Show

In his book *Peak Performers,* Charles Garfield tells the story of a toll taker on the Oakland Bay Bridge: Driving up to the tollbooth one morning, Garfield heard loud rock music and saw that the man inside the booth was dancing. The toll taker gave Mr. Garfield his change without breaking rhythm, smiling as he did so.

Curious, Mr. Garfield returned to interview the man. "I have a corner office," the toll take enthused. "Glass on all sides. I can see the Golden Gate, San Francisco, the Berkeley Hills; half the Western world vacations here, and I just stroll in every day and practice dancing."

The other 16 tollbooths on the bridge were "vertical coffins" where people quietly survived their eight hours a day, the toll taker explained. *He* wanted to become a dancer, and his boss was effectively paying for his practice time in the booth. His mission, an attribute of all peak performers, was to use the job toward his own development beyond it.

26

Learn From Adversity

You may have noticed that life does not always go smoothly. Bad things happen to good people. Good things happen to bad people.

When adversity strikes, remember these ideas:

- We always retain the freedom to choose how we will react. We can fall apart, become consumed with rage, or patiently endure.
- Have faith that there is almost always a silver lining—that something positive can come from even the worst situations.
- Life isn't always fair but things do tend to even out in the long run.
- Every experience we have can be of priceless value. Vow to learn from adversity and, to the degree that it is controllable, to do things differently in the future.
- Don't waste a lot of energy on hate, envy or dreams of revenge.

27

Welcome Criticism

Your worst critic can be your best friend. It's true. Often when people criticize you they provide the information you need to improve yourself. It's like having bad breath. You may be embarrassed when a friend points it out to you, but better that than melting other people's faces when you talk to them.

Let people know that you are open to feedback. Take what they have to say, however painful, sort the emotion out of it, and see what you can apply to improve yourself. People, of course, are not always tactful. Some obnoxious comment may really get your fur up. But try to separate the wheat from the chaff. More often than not, there is at least a grain of truth in even your worst critic's remarks.

It takes a lot of guts to be feedback-receptive, or even better, to ask for negative feedback. Most people would rather keep their heads buried in the sand...but that always leaves one end exposed. Have the humility to accept the fact that you can always improve and that other people may have some good ideas on how to do so.

Try a comment like this: "You seemed to be unhappy with the way I handled ____. If you have a suggestion on how I could have done it better, I'd appreciate it."

Be careful to keep your tone of voice *sincere,* without a trace of sarcasm!

Part 3

Sharpen
Your Vision

28

Take The
Long View

Einstein once said that the greatest power on earth is compound interest. If we invest money in any kind of interest-bearing vehicle, it earns more money. And the money the *money* earns, earns *more* money. You get the picture.

The same principle applies if we consistently "take the long view" and persist in incrementally improving every aspect of our lives. If we do just one thing each day that leads to long-term satisfaction, our ultimate long-term goals will inevitably be met.

It helps to start early in developing that habit. If teen-agers can put a few dollars into a safe investment each month, they can retire at 50...easily. But most teenagers take a shorter view, to put it charitably—most can't imagine themselves *being* 50. They *can* imagine spending their money on a car or other toys.

Part of the long view is to recognize that life has many cycles. What goes around really does come around. The older we get, the clearer this fact becomes.

In terms of your job or career, taking the long view may mean going back to school to learn a new skill or taking a "demotion" to get into a new department that promises greater growth.

The seeds we plant today will inevitably bear fruit later. Good fruit or bad, *something* will sprout.

29

Follow
Your Bliss

There is great power in doing what you love.

Two ways to apply that power at work: Get a job you love, or love the job you have. If you've been doing your job for a long time and you've always hated it—despite constant effort to make it enjoyable or, at the very least, satisfying—you're in the wrong job.

A look inward can help you decide if the job is salvageable. Try a daily activity inventory: List the specific activities you spend your day doing in the left column of a sheet of paper. Then describe your honest feelings about each of these actions in the right column.

Be brutally frank. If you really don't mind something, or get an unexplainable sense of satisfaction out of even the most mundane tasks, write that down. (Remember my earlier example of kind of enjoying washing pots and pans? That may sound crazy to you, but I found it satisfying!) If you really don't care for something, even though others might think that it's exciting or glamorous, write what *you* honestly believe. People often think business travel, for example, is glamorous. Many frequent travelers actually find it frustrating, difficult and exhausting.

Check your self-inventory. Then figure out ways to restructure the job to make it more enjoyable. Share your ideas with your boss. Or start looking for another opportunity.

30

Maintain A Balance

Imagine your life as a three-legged stool. One leg represents your career or job, another your personal development, the third your family or relationships. If each leg isn't carrying some weight, the stool falls.

Many people get hung up on their careers. They spend too much time, effort and resources in building a career while ignoring their personal well-being (health, emotional and spiritual growth) and relationships.

This emphasis can change as we go through life. Young people often invest disproportionate time and effort in a new job or venture, but when they decide to start a family, their emphasis may quickly shift.

Middle-agers are often caught between the demands of teenage or college-age children and the need to take care of aging parents. Working women constantly face the challenges of juggling home, childcare and work responsibilities.

To maintain sanity, strive for balance. Go back to that value system. Remember what's most important and let those values guide your decisions.

A better balance, even if it *seems* to mean less emphasis on career areas, can often result in a healthier, more successful outlook for the career "leg" of your life.

31

Strive To Be Totally Ethical & Honest

The most successful people base their behavior on what they inherently know is right and wrong, not what the "rules" may or may not allow them to do. Use good judgement, treat people fairly and you will build your value—to yourself, your family, your community and, of course, your company.

What's the downside of not being ethical? Stealing paper clips or postage stamps or fudging on an expense account is incredibly short-sighted. Most of us would never dream of shoplifting, yet we regularly "borrow" stuff from the company. Every fall when school begins, companies see a marked increase in requests for office supplies. Gee, I wonder why?

"Shrinkage" (petty theft by customers and/or employees) is a huge problem for retailers. Many a clerk's job has been lost for a few dollars worth of stolen soft drinks or candy bars. The bottom line: Stealing is incredibly stupid. The short-term gains will haunt you. The long-term gains don't exist.

Don't fall into the trap of rationalizing unethical actions. Don't tell yourself that it's OK to make a few personal long-distance calls or run off some photocopies or fudge on an expense account because (sound familiar?): everybody does it; the company doesn't pay very well and

and you deserve some little "perks"; nobody ever checks these things; and/or it won't have any effect on anyone.

Knowing that *you* don't do unethical things increases your self-esteem. If you have done them in the past (and almost everyone has), make a commitment to yourself to quit now.

32
Eliminate
Value Conflicts

Select one of the core values we talked about back in Tactic 19. Write the name of this value on the left side of a sheet of paper. Describe, using the present tense, what it would be like to be congruent with that value. In other words, what would you do, think, and feel like when you've made this value a guiding part of your life?

Take your time. Visualize what your life will be like when you are really at peace with, and totally in-tune with, that value. You probably aren't there yet, but writing the descriptions in the present tense will help you envision getting there.

Here is an example. Suppose "financial security" is one of your key values. What exactly does this mean to you? Here's a serviceable definition: I have sufficient income to provide all the necessities and a few luxuries for my family. I have planned for my retirement and will have a comfortable lifestyle throughout my life. I can afford a nice home, a new car every four years and a two-week vacation each year with my family. I am debt-free. My professional skills will assure me of a good job whenever I need one.

Note that you need not have reached such a goal. You may still have some debts and your home may not be exactly what you'd like right now, but you are moving toward the realization of these statements.

Here's a summary of the three steps in basic value shaping: 1. Name the value; 2. describe (in present tense) what it feels like to be congruent; 3. describe the actions you will take to align yourself with these values. These activities become your personal goals.

A personal value is like the foundation of a building. The goals we set and the things we do will be productive only to the extent that they are built on this foundation. Failure to create a linkage between goals and their values runs the risk of our living life by wandering around—of setting goals that have no permanent attachment to our values. Such goals are hollow and provide little lasting satisfaction.

33

Develop The E-Plus Habit

E-Plus (exceeding expectations) is really a master key to all success. Here is how to apply it: 1. View everyone you deal with as a customer; 2. anticipate what they expect from you; and then, 3. exceed those expectations in some small way.

By doing this, we build in others a sense of obligation to us. Think about it. What stores do you go back to regularly? What restaurants? What medical or dental services? Financial institutions? Your willingness to return to the same places of business probably stems from your sense of satisfaction with those businesses.

What makes for customer satisfaction? Expectations met and exceeded—you feel that you get a *good deal*. Anytime we get a little more from a relationship than we expected, we feel a desire to give more back to that relationship.

Apply the E-Plus approach to everyone you work with—your boss, peers, assistants and clients—and you are bound to increase your value to your company.

34

Be Loyal

Charlie Jones writes, "A lot of people think that loyalty is something you give because of what somebody gave you. That's not loyalty. Loyalty is something you give regardless of what you get back, and in giving loyalty you're getting more loyalty. And out of loyalty flows other great qualities."

Decide which people and organizations deserve your loyalty. Then give it...unconditionally.

- **Relationships:** The outcome of the first three affects the fourth. As we follow the first three R's, we become more caring of others and come to recognize that little can be accomplished—or is *worth* accomplishing—without friends (or, at work, the "team"). Personal effectiveness is impossible without strong relationships—no person can be truly effective alone.

36
Know Your Company's Business

Learn all you can about the company's history, its achievements, its failures and its goals. Take advantage of opportunities to ask top management about their plans. If the company has an open "Q and A" forum in its newsletter or if managers invite questions from employees, always have a pertinent question to ask.

Read everything you can get your hands on that explains the relationships among divisions, departments and subsidiaries. Look for strong and weak points in the organization, in case you need to find another position.

Let it be known that you're available for taking on new challenges. Ideally, you want to maneuver yourself into a department that's a hotbed of promotions and growth.

Part 4

Increase Your Effectiveness

37

Empower Yourself Through Daily Planning

A well-designed planner can add tremendous power to your ability to be productive. In fact, people who begin using a planner system for the first time often report 25-percent boosts in their productivity, almost instantly.

Rule number 1 in the planning process is this: Use *some* kind of a planner, *any* kind of planner. Just find the one that works for *you*. Planning is an individualized activity—we all do it a little differently.

Look for these five things in whatever planner you decide to use:

1. A place to list and assign priorities to tasks for each day.

2. A place to record notes and follow-up information.

3. A place for goals and values. If these are right there for review, you'll pull them into your everyday action planning.

4. A place for frequently referred-to information, especially addresses, phone numbers, important dates.

5. Flexibility to meet your needs. Don't get stuck into some rigid process that may not be useful for you.

A report published in an executive newsletter stated: "As a general rule, spending only 5 percent of the day planning can help managers achieve 95 percent of their goals." Planning helps us avoid doing the wrong things the wrong way at the wrong time, and it forces us to answer the question, "What *really* needs to be accomplished *right now?*" The whole process of time management is one of determining how to do things one at a time, in logical sequence.

Devote 10 or 15 minutes a day to planning. Use these steps:

1. Develop A Priority Task List For Each Day

List in your planner everything that you need to do on that particular day, ranging from the monumental to the trivial, from the optional to the required. But jot things down. Be sure that the planner you select has room to list at least a dozen or more items for each day. Use your own "shorthand"—as long as you are sure you'll be able to recognize it when you read it.

Don't be concerned with the importance of the items just yet; get in the habit of listing everything.

2. Assign A Letter To Each Item On The List —A, B, C, or * (star)

Put the letter A next to items that *must* be done. Tasks that are required, either by outside forces like your boss or by internal ones like your personal commitment, will normally receive an A priority.

Use the letter B to indicate *"should do"* items. They are worth spending time on but aren't as critical as the As.

The letter C is used for *"could do"* items—worth listing, worth thinking about, and if you get the As and Bs all done, worth doing.

The star (*) indicates an item that is *urgent*—something that *must* be done *now*. These tasks are often not anticipated—they crop up unexpectedly during the day. Add them to your list, put a star by them, and drop whatever else you're doing—even if it's an A item—to rush off and get that starred one completed.

3. Assign A Number To Each Task

Use the numbering system as a chronological indicator—that is, which one can you realistically get to first? If you have a crucial meeting at 2:00 p.m. and it's an "A" item, it may not be "A-1", simply because there are other things you'll want to do before 2:00 p.m.

This numbering system provides your marching orders. It tells you how you're going to attack the items that need to be done.

As you complete the tasks listed in your planner, you deserve a reward—a completion symbol. Here they are, starting with the one that feels the best:

(✔) The task has been completed. I prefer to put my check marks all in red just to remind myself of just how productive I've been (colorful, huh?).

(➜) The task needs to be rescheduled, for whatever reason. Perhaps a meeting has been postponed or an appointment changed. Perhaps an activity you were hoping to get to simply could not be done because you were wrapped up in something else.

IMPORTANT: Any time you use the arrow, it is critical to reschedule the task to another day (and, of course, write the new date and time in your planner). When you do this, you earn the right to forget about that task for awhile. It'll come up automatically on the new day you scheduled.

(O) A task that has been delegated to someone else. If you have several people to whom you delegate, you may want to use the circle but put the initial of the person to whom the task is delegated inside it. When the task has been completed by that person, put the check mark in the column.

(X) A task that has been deleted. (Crossing out the whole item is certainly a logical alternative.)

There are two other sections that should appear on your daily pages if you are to get the most from a planner. One is a "schedule" or "appointments" section, the other a "notes" section.

The schedule section is a place where you can indicate specific activities that need to be done at dedicated times. For example, if you have a meeting at 10:00 a.m., write it down.

Your notes section is the place for you to jot down any commitments that have been exchanged with others— telephone calls, ideas, thoughts, or any other bits of information—that may come in handy at some future time. I strongly encourage you to use the note section liberally.

The trick to making priority planning work is to stick to your plan as much as is reasonable. Some people have a tendency to pick up their planner for the day, go through this whole process, take a look at A-1 and say, "Well, I really don't feel like doing that. Let me just take a peek here at A-2 (or A-3 or B-1)." And zoom, before you know it, they're down to C-13, but they never finished A-1, their (supposedly) most important task of all! They're focusing their time on the irrelevant, ignoring the essential. Here is a definition of a successful day: whenever you accomplished every A task on your list!

Don't make the system too complicated. Don't create a monster. View your planner as a useful, helpful friend that will prevent tasks, ideas and thoughts from dropping into the black hole of disorganization where most people live.

38

Use The Power Of Goals

Too often people oversimplify goal-setting, confusing it with wishing or daydreaming. Every skill is learned one step at a time. Success literally breeds success. Little wins lead to more and bigger victories. Goal setting works because goals give direction to life. They provide points of reference. And they teach us self-mastery.

A goal becomes a powerful force when it meets six criteria. Effective goals—the kind that really do motivate—should be:

- *Concrete* and *specific*.

- *Vivid* and exciting to our senses.

- *Realistic*—they should stretch us, but not beyond the bounds of what is reasonable.

- *Measurable* in some quantitative and/or qualitative way, including target dates.
- *Written*—an unrecorded goal is only a wish.
- *Value-anchored.*

Concrete and specific goals are ones that conjure up clear pictures in your mind. The goals should be phrased as positive statements:

Poor phrasing: Lose weight.

Better phrasing: Have a lean body of 121 pounds by September 1.

Avoid negative wording because the mind cannot comprehend a negative. For example, if I told you: "Do not think of an elephant," what's the first thing that pops into your mind? Sure, the elephant. Being even more clear will still not help if the thought is still phrased as a negative: "Do not think of a large yellow elephant with pink polka dots dancing on his hind legs" will still conjure up an instant picture, in part because it is so vivid.

Likewise, a negative statement never conveys as much information as a positive one. If I say "She does *not* live on Main Street," what information do you have? Sure, you can eliminate one possible place where you thought she might live, but you're still in the dark as to where she *does* live. For clarity, use *positive* statements. And the more *specific* the statement, the better: "She lives at 321 Maple Street, Apartment 4-B" would work nicely.

A powerful goal is also one that you can mentally see, hear, touch, taste, feel and even smell. The more of your senses that can be stimulated by the goal, the more powerful the goal.

77

For example, suppose your goal is to become a manager in your company. What will that be like? To make your goal powerful, you need to vividly imagine exactly how it will be. What will you feel like when you come to work in your new role? What will the office be like? What colors, textures, smells, sounds and sights will you experience?

Be realistic. We want our goals to be ambitious so we don't pre-limit our true potential. Yet we also want to be realistic so that the goals don't become a farce.

The result of unrealistic expectations is frustration. When we expect too much from ourselves or from others, we are setting ourselves up for failure.

How can you tell if a goal is realistic? Several questions can give you an inkling:

- Is what I want within the realm of my ability, as I have experienced it in the past?
- Is the desired outcome subject to the problem of scarcity? (Is there enough of the desired goal to go around or few enough people competing for it?)
- Am I honestly willing to pay the price to achieve the desired outcome?

Realistic expectations are powerful propellants to success. Irrational expectations are seeds of folly and disappointment. As H. L. Mencken put it, "The most costly of all follies is to believe passionately in the palpably not true."

We cannot achieve everything we want by just writing down a goal and thinking about it. We are all limited to some degree by natural forces. We may, for example, come up short in body coordination, thus ruling out a career as a professional athlete. Likewise, we all differ in our mental capacity and ways of thinking. Sometimes these natural limitations block us from being something we think we'd like to be.

This does not mean that you should set your goals low. Not at all. I suggest only that you temper them with a dose of reality—not pessimism or small thinking, just reality. Besides, once you've achieved today's realistic goals, you can set new, higher goals for next year. If you want to be president, let's get elected to the city council first.

OK, you've decided that a goal is doable, now what? The next characteristic of a good goal is *measurability*. Measurable goals are more powerful than nonmeasurable. To say you'd like to weigh 160 pounds is more measurable than to simply say, "I'd like to lose some weight."

But be careful here. All things cannot be easily measured with a number, and just because they can't doesn't mean they should not be goals. I've known people who set goals such as "to be more at ease when speaking before groups" or "to feel closer to my spouse." These can be good goal areas even though you can't gauge your progress "by the numbers." Typically, however, these qualitative goals are definable by some specific behaviors—actions that *can* be measured.

A *deadline* is to a goal what a trigger is to a gun. People accomplish more when a deadline looms—they suddenly feel a sense of urgency that propels them toward accomplishment. According to management studies, 80 percent of monthly goals are typically accomplished in the last eight days of a month.

Ultimately, for each of your goals, there should be some action you can take *today*. If financial security is an important goal, do something toward it today: Open a bank account, pay something toward a debt, or decide to toss all your loose change into a can each day—starting *today*.

The power of goals lies in the ways they plant ideas in your mind. To do so requires repetition—programming that computer between our ears. We repeat ideas to ourselves and reinforce our direction by reading our *written* goals. If not written, the goal will change and eventually blow away like a summer cloud.

Finally, a goal must be anchored in a *value*. We achieve a comfortable marriage of values and goals by doing *value-aligning activities*. Since our values come from deep within, they provide exceptional motivation for goal accomplishment.

Let's tie this all in more clearly with saving your job. Real success, satisfaction, and your value as an employee come from setting and attaining objectives that can serve the mutual needs of you and your organization. Motivator Denis Waitley calls it the "double win:" "If I help others in my company win, I win, too."

39

Build & Use
Your Network

Build a file of people you know. Keep their business cards. Look for opportunities to keep in touch.

I knew a very successful man who kept a card file on everybody he'd ever met. On 3" x 5" cards he'd write their names (or staple business cards) and then add personal notes—the names of their spouses, kids, pets. He'd note their interests and hobbies, jokes they may have told, brief experiences they had, the kinds of cars or houses they owned, etc. In short, anything that could be useful in future conversations.

When he read something in a newspaper or magazine in which he thought one of his contacts might be interested, he'd photocopy the clipping and send it with a note. When talking on the phone with someone, he'd have the person's card in front of him. This impressed the heck out of people! To be remembered in such detail conveys that you value the person. Nothing strengthens a network like this attention to detail.

And by maintaining strong relationships with people connected to your industry—whether as clients, vendors, consultants or associates—you increase your value to your employer. Instead of employing one effective worker— you—your boss benefits from the expertise of hundreds of others—your well-maintained network!

40
Know When To
Ask For Help

When to ask for help can be a sensitive matter. Sometimes you are stumped and really need some clarification or fresh ideas. Sometimes all you really need (and want) is reassurance that you are on the right track. If you need help, get it; if you are just fishing for a compliment, skip it.

Be sensitive to your boss's style. Some bosses want to be deeply involved in a project, and they use requests for help as an opportunity to teach their subordinates. (Does your boss seem to get a kick out of teaching?)

Others only want to see the final product and not be bothered with frequent questions. A bank executive once told me, "Some subordinates will take an assignment, work as hard as possible, then come back to you when they get stuck or when it is completed. Other people start coming back to you to do their work for them. People in the second group don't do very well at our bank."

If you think the boss wants to know what you are doing as you progress, send her a brief progress report. If you really need help, be prepared for specific suggestions that your boss feels would allow you to complete the work. Never go to the boss with a vague, unfocused request for "help"—that really sounds like you'd like to bail out of the job.

41

Create A Personal Board Of Advisers

Every now and then, you are likely to face a problem or challenge you've had no experience with. These are times when you need a board of advisers—people whose experience and opinions you trust. (If you've built up your network, you've already got some great candidates!)

To be ready for such times, make a list in advance. Who would you go to for advice about:

- How to dress for a banquet?
- Legal problems?
- Taxes and financial planning?
- Computer problems?
- Job techniques?
- Career planning?
- Dealing with difficult customers/co-workers/bosses?

You get the idea. You may want to let each of these people know that you see him or her as your "guru" on a particular topic and that you appreciate his or her advice and guidance.

If your advisers can't help with a particular problem, ask for their ideas on who to turn to next. They undoubtedly have advisers, too!

42

Promote Yourself With "FYI" Notes

Public relations is the art of doing things and letting people know about them. Consider doing your own "PR."

You don't need to brag. Instead, use simple techniques to let your boss know what you've been able to accomplish. If, for example, you just untangled a sticky billing problem for a customer, send your supervisor an "FYI" (For Your Information) note:

> *Boss: As you know, we've been having a major problem with Mrs. Pim's account. Here's what I did: [Describe the actions taken] I hope this solves the problem. If you have any other ideas or directions on how to better deal with similar situations in the future, please let me know.*

This note does several things. First, it keeps the boss informed. Second, it displays some action you've taken. And third, it expresses your openness to feedback from him or her.

Don't report everything you do, just the exceptional work. Often, a supervisor will keep such notes in your personnel file and, when performance review time comes around, will be reminded of just how valuable you are.

43

Delegate As Much As You Can

Everyone can and should delegate some tasks. Delegate whenever others can do a task more *efficiently*, more *cheaply* or simply *better* than you.

You are delegating, for example, when you decide to run your car through the automatic car wash instead of going home, dragging out the bucket and hose, and doing it yourself. You're trading a few dollars for some valuable time.

You're delegating when you ask your spouse to pick up a gallon of milk on the way home from work.

Or when you ask an office worker to drop off a letter at the post office (which she passes on her way home).

As you take on additional organizational responsibilities, delegation becomes even more important. Sometimes it's a pain—it often seems easier to just do the job yourself than to spend *more* time teaching someone else how to do it.

But over the long run, delegation and teaching others makes great sense.

As one old saying puts it, "Lazy parents pick up after their children." Teach others to do it themselves (i.e., delegate the job to them), and you'll multiply your effectiveness.

44
Do It Now

Nothing impresses anyone as much as immediate follow up.

If you say you'll do something, do it *now*.

E-Plus your boss, coworker, subordinate or customer with quicker action than he or she expects.

One day I was talking with another manager in his office about where we could get some lawn-care product we needed. We talked about a store where we could get it and I made a mental note to stop by there "someday" and check it out.

The other fellow, Jim, decided to do it now. He picked up the phone, called about the product, and arranged to have it delivered...while I was still thinking about it!

45
Use A "Ready-Fire-Aim" Action Mode

The late Sam Walton, founder of Wal-Mart, was a great one for trying new things. He recommended that his managers at all levels take initiative, try new ideas. Follow his example: When you have a promising idea, just try it, fix the parts that don't work, and implement it.

A lot of people analyze ideas to death.

Obviously if you're doing brain surgery, you'd better plan it out in detail. But short of that, most ideas can be fixed as you go.

Make your ideas like guided missiles. Fire them in the general direction of the target and let the feedback and control mechanisms make the necessary adjustments to get you there.

46

Beat
Procrastination

There are four reasons for procrastinating:

- Fear of failure
- Fear of success
- Lack of discipline
- To express rebelliousness

Decide which reason *you* are using, then change it. Do the worst job first each day (if it's an A priority) and then enjoy the good feeling of having it accomplished.

47

Handle Paperwork
Quickly

The best rule for handling paperwork is to handle each paper only once. Be decisive. Determine which of these four actions you should take:

1. File it away for future reference.
2. Refer it to someone else.

3. Act upon it now (e.g., answer it with a quick, handwritten note).
4. Trash it.

48

De-Junk Your
Work Area

William R. Bradford said, "A cluttered life is a life that you do not have control of. It is a life in which the things you have surrounded yourself with are controlling you."

A few minutes (or even hours) spent now to clean up clutter and trash unneeded stuff can make you feel more productive for days. But don't just transfer things from one place to another. Really sort it out. You'll never miss it. (95 percent of the things people keep in their files are never again referred to. So start with your files.)

49

Maintain Two-Way Trust
With Your Boss

Four conditions are necessary for subordinate-superior trust to develop: accessibility, availability, predictability and loyalty.

An **accessible** person takes in ideas easily and gives them out freely. If two people are going to develop a productive relationship, they must respect each other's ideas and give those ideas careful thought and consideration. A subordinate who does not respect the boss's ideas will never be trusted nor obtain the needed help to develop his or her own ideas.

A subordinate should be **attentive** and **available** physically, mentally, and emotionally when the manager is under pressure and needs support.

The **predictable** person handles the loose ends thoroughly and consistently. Predictability also means reliability in reaching important deadlines and doing high quality work.

Personal **loyalty** to one's boss and from boss to subordinate is important. Trust is damaged when either party in the relationship fears that the other has hidden motives. You don't have to be crazy about your supervisor or subordinates, but you *should* feel an obligation of loyalty to them as long as they are working toward the legitimate goals of the organization.

50

Use Humor, When Appropriate

Used effectively, humor on the job not only increases your personal and professional effectiveness, but also the effectiveness of others. Humor serves to disarm anger, unlock the receptivity of others, diffuse resistance to change, and promote problem solving.

People who develop a healthy sense of humor can develop more self-confidence and manage stress in a changing world.

Some argue that humor can help an organization run smoother, cut medical costs, increase sales and productivity, even polish the company's public image. And best of all, it doesn't cost a penny.

Humor contributes to the culture of an organization, as long as it's kept wholesome. Humor that belittles or annoys does no good for anyone.

Avoid ethnic or sexist jokes or quips.

51

Keep Clarifying Expectations

Regularly clarify job-content expectations. Especially when the company is rapidly changing, be sure you and your manager are on the same wavelength. A written job description can be a good starting point, but it can easily become obsolete. Periodically checking—and rechecking— with your manager will avoid misunderstandings.

Know the limits of your responsibilities and authority. If in doubt about these, ask for clarification. In a clarification meeting, have specific questions written out in advance so you don't just ramble.

52

Live An
E-Plus Life

Surprise! I've just exceeded your expectations of this *book* by providing you with a *52nd* tip, even though I promised only 51.

Exceeding your customers' expectations is the master key to *all* success—including success in saving your job.

Who are your "customers"? Anyone you deal with—within the company, externally, even your personal relationships. Constantly look for ways to exceed what people expect from you. Give a little *more,* a little *faster,* a little *better* service than they expect.

We can't give away more than we get back. There is, I firmly believe, a natural law that brings back to us all that we give to others...and more. We attract to ourselves the spirit of service, caring, loyalty and quality if *we* project that spirit.

Ultimately, we save our jobs—and enrich our lives—to the degree that we willingly choose to serve above and beyond the barest minimum society requires.

Think E-Plus.

And live it.

It pays off.

Index